THE SCHOOL OF MARY

Meditations on the
Mysteries of the Rosary

The
SCHOOL OF MARY

Meditations on the
Mysteries of the Rosary

⊕

Monsignor Florian Kolfhaus

Translated by
Michaela Mineo

 Angelico Press

First published in Italian as
Il rosario. Teologia in ginocchio
© Edizioni Cantagalli, 2014
First published in English by Angelico Press, 2016
English translation © Michaela Mineo, 2016

For information, address:
Angelico Press, Ltd.
4709 Briar Knoll Dr.
Kettering, OH 45429
www.angelicopress.com

ISBN: 978-1-62138-162-4 pbk
ISBN: 978-1-62138-163-1 ebook

Cover Design: Michael Schrauzer
Cover Image: Duccio di Buoninsegna
Maestà 1308–1311 (detail)

CONTENTS

THE JOYFUL MYSTERIES

THE LUMINOUS MYSTERIES

THE SORROWFUL MYSTERIES

THE GLORIOUS MYSTERIES

Introduction

he Churches of the East call the apostle and evangelist John the "theologian." They bestowed this honorary title upon him not only because his Gospel, as suggested by his symbol, the eagle, soars high up to the contemplation of God and represents the mystery of the Incarnation of the *Logos* in a clearer way than Matthew, Mark, and Luke, but because he, the beloved disciple, rested on Jesus's chest at the Last Supper (Jn 13:25; 21:20). He is a theologian, a knower of the sacred science, since he studied Jesus, not by reading erudite books but by listening to His heart. John, the only apostle present at Golgotha, indeed sees this heart pierced. He looks into the very depths of the Redeemer to recognize, as he will later write, that "God is love" (1 Jn 4:8). John, the theologian, becomes Mary's son under the Cross. Jesus entrusts him to His mother and conversely commends the Virgin to John's care. The house in Ephesus, where John and Mary live, becomes the school of the theologians: the Mother opens her soul to the disciple, telling him all the wonderful things that she had kept and pondered in her heart (Lk 2:19; 2:51). The apostle learns from Mary, who understands Jesus better than all His disciples, and in such a broader way that all the books of the world could not possibly contain what should be written (cf. Jn 21:25).

1

Theology, as St. Thomas Aquinas (1225–1274) writes, is the science of the saints.[1] He does not mean that all those who dedicate themselves to this study are saints, but that they imitate those who contemplate God in heaven. That which the blessed receive immediately in the *visio beatifica*, the vision of God—namely, the deep understanding of the Holy Trinity—is what the theologian on earth with the intellect illuminated by faith tries to understand when he studies revelation as transmitted by the Church. There exists an academic theology that is indispensable in demonstrating that faith and reason are not in opposition. It uses the scientific method and follows the rules of logic to explain, defend, and deepen what the Church teaches. In this respect, not every Christian can be a theologian, but every theologian must be a believing

1 St. Thomas Aquinas, *Summa Theologiae*: "I answer that, Sacred doctrine is a science. We must bear in mind that there are two kinds of sciences. There are some which proceed from a principle known by the natural light of intelligence, such as arithmetic and geometry and the like. There are some which proceed from principles known by the light of a higher science: thus the science of perspective proceeds from principles established by geometry, and music from principles established by arithmetic. So it is that sacred doctrine is a science because it proceeds from principles established by the light of a higher science, namely, the science of God and the blessed. Hence, just as the musician accepts on authority the principles taught him by the mathematician, so sacred science is established on principles revealed by God" (I, q. 1, a. 2).

Christian who lets himself be guided and often corrected in this search for God by the light of revelation and the teaching of the Church. Without vibrant faith, theology becomes at best a science of religion, a study of history or biblical literary criticism: important disciplines that can, however, be taught excellently even by non-Christians. In the worst case scenario, the theologian commits the error, arising mostly from blind pride, of believing that he, better than the Magisterium of the Church, the inspired authors of the Holy Scriptures, or the great masters of the past, knows what faith is and how it should be lived today, even when this knowledge is in conflict with the teachings of the Church. A theologian misses his higher vocation when he no longer goes down on his knees, making himself little and therefore recognizing that his intellect can understand much but still needs the grace of God in order to enter into the great mystery of faith, without ever comprehending it completely. Science basically strives for a higher knowledge, just as theology does. However, the knowledge of the revelation of God is not an end unto itself; rather, it urges us toward worship, praise, thanks, and, not least, to the service of His kingdom. In that respect, Cardinal Journet (1891–1975) repeatedly claims that theology must open itself to mysticism, but not through the quest for extraordinary phenomena or the betrayal of the principles of science, which could lead to fideism or religious sentimentalism. He suggests that the knowledge of truth helps us to take the leap toward astonishment at beauty and to do good things.[2] For this reason, for the theologian and his work, what St. Teresa of Avila (1515–1582) said about prayer is valid: "The important thing is not to think much but to love much."[3] The more I know about Jesus, understand His lessons, and can immerse myself in the mysteries of His life and my redemption, the more I will love Him gratefully and make every effort to make Him recognized and loved by others. This love, as St. Maximilian Kolbe (1894–1941) says, is learned only on one's knees.[4]

Although not every Christian can be considered a theologian in the sense of being a scholar, all Christians should still study Jesus the way the apostle John did: resting on Jesus's heart, looking at the pierced side of the Redeemer and letting Jesus's mother tell them about His life. More

2 Cf. G. Boissard, R. Latala, J. Rime, *Charles Journet et Nova et Vetera*: "Theology stands under the prayer. I don't believe we have to penetrate it deeply in order to pray well. A little child can pray in a wonderful way" (translated by the author).

3 St. Teresa of Avila, *The Interior Castle*: "I only wish to inform you that in order to profit by this path and ascend to the dwelling places we desire, the import thing is not to think much but to love much; and so do that which best stirs you to love" (fourth mansion, chapter 1.7).

4 St. Maximilian Kolbe: "In obedience the Immaculate shows us her will. Praying on one's knees, one can learn more about the Mother of God than from the most erudite books" (from *The Writings of St. Maximilian Kolbe*, translated by the author).

so than in previous eras, nowadays the study of the Holy Scriptures and the catechism is necessary in order to learn the teachings of the Church. Furthermore, it is essential to be connected in a deeper and more intimate way with Jesus. We are not studying the legendary actions of the mythical Ulysses, but rather the One who is alive and loves us. Prayer is necessary in order to know Him. A theology that "gets down on its knees" is needed to understand inwardly that Jesus is not merely one of the great men of the past whose example continues to affect us; rather, He is the Living One whose words I hear every time I turn to Him. Marthe Robin (1902–1981) expresses this concept in a pure, clear way with the following words: "My science is love. Sometimes I envy those who have the good fortune to be theologians! But doesn't prayer—divine contemplation—soar much higher in knowledge, love and power, than the highest studies? Feeling is deeper, more luminous, and more fruitful than science. As far as I am concerned, my theology—my science—is love, the union of my heart with God's through Jesus Christ and the Blessed Virgin. Nothing more and nothing less!"[5] Where and how is it possible to study this "kneeling theology"? Where is the academy that teaches this sacred science? Which professor invites

5 From *Prends Ma Vie Seigneur* [Take My Life Lord] by Raymond Peyret.

his students, in order to guide them, to imitate St. John the theologian?

Saint Louis-Marie Grignion de Montfort (1673–1716) is firmly convinced that the best master of Christ is His mother Mary. She is, as he calls her in his work about total consecration to Jesus through Mary, popularly known as the Golden Book, an "easy, short, perfect, and safe road to perfection, which means union with Christ. To a Christian, perfection is nothing else than such a union."[6] Her school, through which the Mother shows us her Son, is the rosary. He who prays it, studies "theology on its knees." In fact, the rosary was born from the desire to look at Jesus with and through Mary in order to know and love Him better. Already the Hail Mary, the greeting of the angel and the praise of Elizabeth, turns our attention to the center of the history of the world and of salvation: the Son of God becomes man thanks to the "yes" of the Virgin of Nazareth.

The order of the Beguines of Ghent in 1242 demanded already, in line with the 150 psalms, the daily prayer of 150 Hail Marys. It would be narrow-minded to consider it a quantitative performance that could be carried out as rapidly as possible. The continuous repetition, a spiritual experience shared by many religions, deepens and throws

6 St. Louis-Marie Grignion de Montfort, *True Devotion to the Blessed Virgin Mary*, Montfort Publications, p. 61.

light on the contemplated mystery that, like the Incarnation of the Son of God, remains always inexhaustible. Whereas the prayer of the Hail Mary was initially called the Marian psalter, in the High Middle Ages the concept of the rosary developed to express that the prayer weaves a spiritual crown for the Mother of God. Nowadays, using this symbol in reference to the three parts of the Marian psalter, we could add that while praying the joyful mysteries the believer picks white roses, for the sorrowful mysteries red, and for the glorious mysteries golden-yellow. These remind us of the crown that the Lord placed on the head of the Mother in heaven; with this prayer we give her our own crown. These mysteries go back in a comprehensive form to Dominic of Prussia, who invented as a novice 150 *clausulae* (short meditations) in 1409 and inserted them into the Hail Mary after Jesus's name in order to draw attention in an easier way to Jesus's life. As such, to stay with the metaphor, he intertwined an even more colorful wreath with different flowers. There is, however, disagreement as to when the mysteries were simplified to fifteen for a total of fifty Hail Marys repeated three times. Probably Adolf of Essen, this young monk's prior, had already summarized the *clausulae* of his disciple. It is certain, however, that by 1483 at the latest the enduring form of this prayer was created.

The rosary is Mary's psalter. Mary herself handed to St. Dominic a string of pearls in a vision and recommended it as the most efficient tool for the conversion of the heretical Albigensians. The strategy of success of the mission and of the new evangelization does not consist in continuously undertaking new actions, useful though they are, but in hoping always more in God's intervention than in human activity, and therefore in turning first to Him.

Wars have been won with the rosary in hand: the battle of Lepanto, whose memory was perpetuated by the introduction of the Feast of the Rosary; the victory over the Turks besieging Vienna, which is still celebrated today as the Holy Name of Mary; and, finally, the peaceful withdrawal of the Russian troops from Austria, for which believers most fervently prayed through the public recitation of the rosary. The rosary with its five mysteries is like David's slingshot and the five little stones: even giants can be defeated! For this reason Blessed Mother Teresa (1919–1997) said once that "there is no problem, no matter how difficult it is, that we cannot solve by the prayer of the Holy Rosary."

The effectiveness of the rosary lies in its simplicity. It is a prayer that can be performed by everyone: children and the elderly, the sick and the healthy, travelers and those confined to the home with little more than an image of Mary to inspire them. In the simplicity of the fifty Hail Marys, which reflect the mysteries of the life of Jesus and of His mother, lies certainly also the great danger of considering the rosary to be a monotone and superficial recitation of prayer forms. In reality, the rosary is an excellent school of prayer, an academy, where Christians learn from the very hands of the Mother, pearl after pearl, step by step, to approach Jesus Christ, to talk with Him, to listen to Him and contemplate Him with love. The holy rosary incorporates the three great forms of prayer that, as steps of a staircase, lead us to an encounter with the Lord: oral prayer, meditation, and contemplation. In other words, the one who recites the rosary prays with the mouth, the intellect, and the heart. He who "recites" only the Hail Mary and considers the rapid recitation of as many words as possible already a good prayer can be compared to a Latin student who conjugates the verbs in chorus with the class but has never opened a book of Latin poets. In the school of Mary, the Hail Mary begins and accompanies the prayer, but the teacher wants to tell us much more.[7]

The prayer of the rosary can be compared perhaps to playing the guitar. We first have oral prayers: the Our Father, the Hail Mary, and the Glory Be. These are the fundamental prayers of Christianity; it can be said that they come almost entirely from heaven, especially considering that the Our Father and the first part of the Hail Mary are found in the inspired texts of the Sacred Scriptures. Often there is a Jesus Prayer, which the Mother of

---

7 See Florian Kolfhaus, *Totus Tuus, Maria: Personal Consecration to Our Lady Following the Spiritual Teaching of St. Louis-Marie Grignion de Montfort*, Gracewing Publishing, 2014.

God revealed at Fatima and which is added to the end of each decade of the rosary. The recitation of these prayers can be compared to the right hand that beats the rhythm when one is holding the guitar. This is not real music yet. Whoever believes that the rosary is only an oral prayer or, in an even worse caricature, an endless rattling off of words, deceives himself like someone who touches the strings of a guitar and considers this already a song. Besides the rhythm, when one is playing the guitar the tones, produced by the left hand, are necessary. And so it is for the rosary: the oral prayers form the framework for the meditation of the mysteries. As when one is playing the guitar the left hand plays the major and minor chords, we get to know the joyful mysteries of Jesus's childhood, the sorrowful ones of His suffering and death, and the glorious ones of His resurrection and glorification.

There are always five chords in the rhythm of the always repeating prayers that show us the life of Jesus and the Virgin Mary. During the meditation we ponder what happens in these mysteries and their meaning in our life.

"In Nazareth the Son of God becomes man in Mary, and in Holy Communion He comes to me too! . . . In Gethsemane Jesus sweats blood. He suffers and is afraid, but His friends are asleep. Do I watch over Him or close my eyes because of my exhaustion? . . . On Easter Sunday Jesus rises from the grave. The first day of creation brought the light. . . . The first day of the week Jesus defeated death and gave us life. He transforms our darkness into light."

Our prayer begins to become music, it is by no means monotone or boring anymore, but rich in images and thoughts and, by God's grace, loaded with enlightenment and supernatural suggestions. The right and the left hand give respectively the rhythm and the chords: these are oral prayer and meditation, mouth and intellect while reciting the rosary.

In order to become really good music and an even deeper and more intimate prayer, another aspect is necessary: the melody sung by the heart. While playing the guitar a voice that sings the song is essential. When praying the rosary the singing of the heart is part of it and offers in the beat of the prayer and mysteries its own life to God. The reflection and meditation become a dwelling in God, with gratitude and petition, praise and repentance, childlike joy or apostolic determination. It is about the singing of the heart, which is set into vibration during the mysteries of the rosary: "You went to visit Mary through Elizabeth—remain in my heart, let me be bearer of Christ as I am also a living tabernacle whenever I receive you in the Eucharist! . . . You were scourged for me. It was me who hit you—again and again. Forgive me! . . . You ascended into heaven, O Lord. I long for you, I long for your kingdom, my real fatherland." In contemplation, the person who prays sees the mystery as it is in front of his eyes and dwells in a particular state of affection and the feeling of his heart before God. He sings his personal melody of love that can and should contain also real personal concerns: "You wanted to become the child of a human mother—help my ill mother! . . . You were crowned with thorns, assist me in my present financial worry that I cannot get out of my head. . . . You sent your Spirit—to help me to make a good decision because without you I have neither strength nor courage."

The rosary is, after the liturgical prayer of the Church, which finds its central and culminating moment in the celebration of the Holy Mass, an excellent instrument not only for personal sanctification but also for the conversion of the world. Therefore, Mary asked at Lourdes and Fatima for the frequent and daily recitation of the rosary. Pope John Paul II insisted on the significance of the rosary in his apostolic letter *Rosarium Virginis* and added the luminous mysteries from Jesus's life. For this reason, the number of Hail Marys, initially inspired by the 150 psalms, was increased to 200.[8] The twenty images that the rosary

---

8 Pope John Paul II, *Rosarium Virginis Mariae*: "Of the many mysteries of Christ's life, only a few are indicated by the Rosary in the form that has become generally established with the seal of the Church's approval. The selection was determined by the origin of the prayer, which was based on the number 150, the number of the psalms in the psalter. I believe, however, that to bring out fully the Christological depth of the Rosary it would be suitable to make an addition to the traditional pattern which, while left to the freedom of individuals and communities, could broaden it to include *the mysteries of Christ's public ministry between his Baptism and his Passion*. In the course of those mysteries we contemplate important aspects of the person of Christ as the definitive revelation of God" (no. 19).

presents to the person who prays are like luminous stained glass windows of a church where the sun of grace breaks through. Mary shows and explains them to us in the same way as mothers who bring their children to a cathedral and, making use of the displayed artwork, tell them about Jesus's life. In the rosary, Mary is like a good teacher who not only tells us about her Son, but also shows Him to us when we look at Him in the contemplation of the mysteries of His life. The theology of the Mother is not an arid and abstract study of books, but a loving insight into all that she wants to show us.

How many humble people have gained a more intimate understanding of belief through the prayer of the rosary than that of some scientists who, though they certainly know the theology of the Holy Trinity and the Sacrament of the Altar, no longer go down on their knees in front of these mysteries. The rosary is "theology on its knees" that consolidates and refines the *sensus fidei*, the sense of faith of every baptized Christian living in grace. It is about imagining and sensing the true, the good, and the beautiful, as the instinct reacts allergically to error and malice without, perhaps, exactly uncovering the error. Again, often it is and it has been the humble who recognize errors in sermons, unworthy incidents in liturgies, or absurd teachings during religious education. As John, the theologian, studied the Master by His side and learned from Him simply by watching and listening to Him, so we learn from Mary's heartbeat. Through this pulse that repeatedly reaches our ear with the regular repetition of the Hail Mary, we learn to love her Son always more and, at the same time, as is typical for lovers, become constantly more aware of and sensitive to that which gives Him joy or displeasure.

Saint Louis-Marie Grignion de Montfort was convinced that the saints are formed in Mary. The "diploma" that can be obtained in the School of Jesus's mother is the sanctity that means a life following or, better, imitating Christ. It is the tragedy of our time that the saint is often caricatured as intolerant and sanctimonious, as one who not only does not know what life is but also does not know how to rejoice in it. The saint appears as a moralizing ascetic, an unworldly eccentric, or a naive dreamer.[9] How wrong is this view of things! So writes St. Teresa Benedicta of the Cross (Edith Stein, 1891–1942) to her sister: "By the way, I believe that it isn't necessary for a saint to renounce all the desires, hopes and joys of the world. On the contrary:

9 Pope Benedict XVI, Vigil with Young People: "Dear friends, again and again the very notion of saints has been caricatured and distorted, as if to be holy meant to be remote from the world, naive and joyless. Often it is thought that a saint has to be someone with great ascetic and moral achievements, who might well be revered, but could never be imitated in our own lives. How false and discouraging this opinion is! There is no saint, apart from the Blessed Virgin Mary, who has not also known sin, who has never fallen" (Freiburg im Breisgau, September 24, 2011).

we are in the world to live and we should gratefully accept the beauty there is."[10] The saints are the ones who are truly happy in this life and the afterlife. The Latin expression beatus (blessed, happy) suggests it already: sanctity is synonymous with the true and lasting happiness for which God created us. In order to not lose sight of this goal, the world needs saints, men and women who keep both feet on the ground of reality yet have heaven in sight. Mary wants to teach us about such persons.

Basically, every man yearns for sanctity, for fellowship with God; for this he was created. Inside each of us burns the yearning to know our reason for being and, when grace moves us, to meet the One who is love. To love and to be loved, and specifically with the dedication that is only possible with God, is the deepest human desire, the fulfillment of what we hope for as happiness and beati-

---

10 Edith Stein (St. Teresa Benedicta of the Cross), in a letter dated February 12, 1928, to Sr. Callista Kopf, a former student of Edith Stein's in Speyer: "Immediately before, and for a good while after my conversion, I was of the opinion that to lead a religious life meant one had to give up all that was secular and to live totally immersed in thoughts of the Divine. But gradually I realized that something else is asked of us in this world and that, even in the contemplative life, one may not sever the connection with the world. I even believe that the deeper one is drawn into God, the more one must 'go out of oneself,' that is, one must go to the world in order to carry the divine life into it" (Edith Stein, *Self-Portrait in Letters* 1916–1942, ed. by L. Gelber and R. Leuven. Washington, DC: Institute of Carmelite Studies, 1993, p. 54).

tude. The human heart is too big to be filled with anything less than God. But what is a saint? Also here there are disastrous and erroneous beliefs that disfigure the true image of sanctity. It is not about morally perfect actions and in no way about a shallow "niceness." Being a saint is, even before our good work begins, a gift of God. "In baptism the Lord, as it were, sets our life alight with what the Catechism calls sanctifying grace. Those who watch over this light, who live by grace, are holy."[11] The aim of our life consists, therefore, in preserving and increasing this grace. Yes, baptism makes us Christians and requires us to live as Christ, hence, to live in sanctity.

The greatest miracle of all occurred in Mary: the Son of God became man. In her we can find, as in a living tabernacle, the Lord. She has formed Christ and can form us to be good Christians in the image of Jesus; she will make saints of us, because being real Christians means exactly this. Saint Maximilian Kolbe even says that "there is no doubt that all the saints are formed by the hands of the Blessed Virgin. Why? Because all the graces flow through the hands of the Holy Mother." Also the Curé of Ars (1786–1859) was firmly convinced that "all the Saints, without exception, have a great devotion to Our Blessed Virgin: no grace comes from Heaven without passing through her hands." Devotion to Mary is by no means of

11 Pope Benedict XVI, Vigil with Young People, Freiburg im Breisgau, September 24, 2011.

secondary importance or even—as some believe—unnecessary. No! "Being Catholic means being Marian."[12]

Again and again, there are people who consider devotion to Mary an exaggeration or an act of nothing other than sentimental piety. *De Maria numquam satis*, respond the believers who entrust themselves to Mary as their mother and teacher: "Of Mary, there is never enough!" In fact, one cannot say too much about Mary. Praising her can truly never be considered an exaggeration. Adoration is due only to God. Mary is and remains a creature, but she is the masterpiece of a divine Artist, and no other created thing can reflect His greatness as she does. Mary is the Mother of God: no other creature can make this statement about itself. She is the only one who can call her Lord and God "my Son"!

Entrusting yourself to Mary and taking her hand during the prayer of the rosary does not mean anything else than entering into the dynamic of love and following the logic of the Incarnation. For this reason, the Hail Mary is repeated so often in the rosary—it reminds us of the moment of the Incarnation of the Son of God. In Nazareth, Jesus and Mary, the new Adam and the new Eve, the Redeemer and His companion, the Son of Man and the

12 See Pope Benedict XVI, Audience with the Delegation of the Marian Congregation for Men "Mariä Verkündigung," Regensburg, May 28, 2011.

Mother of God, bind themselves so closely and intimately, that from the moment of the Incarnation Jesus cannot be found without His mother nor Mary without her Son. What He is by nature, the Virgin is by grace. As theology says that Christ is Lord *de condigno* (with respect to His own dignity) and Mary *de congruo* (by appropriateness), Blessed Bartolo Longo (1841–1926), the great apostle of the rosary, expresses himself in the following way in a prayer to Mary: "You are almighty by grace."[13] For this reason the Church uses the christological titles also in the feminine form for His mother: King—Queen; Mediator—Mediatrix; Savior—Salvatrix; new Adam—new Eve. Saint Catherine of Siena (1347–1380) calls Mary even *Redemptrix*. Mary is so deeply involved in Jesus Christ's work of redemption that truly there is no way other than her that leads to Jesus. Thus, Pope Leo XIII writes the following in *Octobri Mense*: "With equal truth may it be also affirmed that, by the will of God, Mary is the intermediary through whom is distributed unto us this immense treasure of mercies gathered by God, for 'grace and truth were realized by Jesus Christ' (Jn 1:17). Thus as no man goeth to the Father but by the Son, so no man goeth to Christ but by His Mother."[14] As Christ is the

---

13 St. Bartolo Longo, *Intercession of Our Lady of the Rosary of Pompeii*, 1883.

14 Pope Leo XIII, *Octobri Mense*.

only way to the Father also for the ones who do not know and pray to Him because they blamelessly or as a result of insurmountable obstacles have not found Him, so is Mary always and for everyone the gate that gives access to her Son, even for those who do not know her mediation. Saint Gabriel Possenti (1838–1862) says, "I believe that all the graces which God dispenses pass through Mary's hands, and that no one will enter Heaven except through her, who is the Gate of Heaven. I believe that true devotion to Mary is a most certain sign of eternal salvation."[15]

Quite a few theologians propagate a "Marian minimalism" and warn about exaggerations, often on the basis of questionable ecumenical considerations, as if true and sincere love for Mary could displease the Son or even displace Him. Of course, it is possible to disseminate false or erroneous thoughts about the Virgin, as happens nowadays on account of some dubious private revelations from the Virgin, or to obsess over miracles, or to be sensationalistic. Saint Bernardine of Siena preached against tales that were not worthy of the Mother of God and against an excessively superficial devotion. A Franciscan saint who wanted to impede the proliferation of dubious Marian relics, among them Mary's milk that fed baby Jesus, says with his clear and lively voice, seemingly disrespectful

15 See Ferdinand Holböck, *Geführt von Maria: Marianische Heilige aus allen Jahrhunderten der Kirchengeschichte*, Christiana Verlag, 1987, p. 490 (translated by the author).

and delicate at the same time, "Don't run after these relics! The Virgin Mary wasn't a cow! She had only enough milk for the mouth of the little Jesus Christ."

The Second Vatican Council warns in *Lumen Gentium,* no. 67 against "gross exaggerations" and "petty narrow-mindedness,"[16] with emphasis clearly on "gross"; the Council in no way questions the Catholic principle of *de Maria numquam satis* but rather confirms the cult of hyperdulia—excessive praise—reserved only for Mary.[17]

This teaching confirming hyperdulia, as with other teachings of that council, has often been forgotten or concealed. It is not about provoking Protestant brothers and sisters or offending Catholics who know little about Mary. Pastoral wisdom and humble patience are needed when explaining the extraordinary greatness of Jesus's mother. But these considerations clearly should not lead to such "spiritual-mindedness" that we dare not praise Mary effu-

16 See Vatican II, *Lumen Gentium* (Dogmatic Constitution on the Church), no. 67: "But it exhorts theologians and preachers of the divine word to abstain zealously both from all gross exaggerations as well as from petty narrow-mindedness in considering the singular dignity of the Mother of God."

17 Ibid., no. 66: "Placed by the grace of God, as God's Mother, next to her Son, and exalted above all angels and men, Mary intervened in the mysteries of Christ and is justly honored by a special cult in the Church. . . . This cult, as it always existed, although it is altogether singular, differs essentially from the cult of adoration which is offered to the Incarnate Word, as well to the Father and the Holy Spirit, and it is most favorable to it."

sively in our prayers, or recognize her greatness from the pulpit, or devoutly study her unique role as mother and companion of the Redeemer.

The saints never feared that they could exaggerate in praising the Blessed Virgin. They were all, so to speak, "Marian maximalists," following the principle of Blessed Duns Scotus (1266–1308): "We can with probability attribute to Mary all that has the greatest perfection, provided it is not opposed to the authority of the Church or the Scriptures."[18] The students of the Mother of God who want to "study" Jesus at her feet call themselves Mary's children, her servants, her slaves, her property, as if they want to surpass each other in their gift of self. Saint John Eudes (1601–1680) even says, "If I knew a person who loves Mary more than me, I would hurry there, even a hundred miles, to learn from him how to love the Virgin even more."

The rosary is "theology on its knees" that is learned by the ones who pray in the school of Mary. However, this is so only if they let themselves be led from the Mother to the Son and trust her blindly without excessive spiritual-mindedness. He who prays with such filial devotion will always more deeply recognize the great mysteries of our faith and look with astonishment at the beauty of the

---

18 Duns Scotus, *Ord.* III, d. 3, q. 1, no. 32: "Si auctoritati Ecclesiae, vel auctoritati Scripturae non repugnat, videtur probabile quod excellentius est, attribuire Mariae."

work of redemption. Yes, the rosary is beautiful, as it shows us Jesus and Mary, new Adam and Eve, crown of all creation. The rosary teaches us to admire their beauty and to love them always more.

Bernard of Cluny (France, twelfth century) is the author of the famous Marian hymn *Omni Die Dic Mariae*, composed around the year 1140. He highlights the Christian's inability to sing praise worthy of Mary: *Nullus certe tam disertae, exstat eloquentiae: Qui condignos promat hymnos eius excellentiae*—"Never was it possible for someone to sing of her great dignity. God Himself has raised her to His majesty."[19] The hymn was one of the favorite ones of St. Casimir of Poland (1458–1484), a zealous devotee of Mary. He loved the words of this poetic composition so much that he ordered this text written on his tomb. Saint Thomas Aquinas wrote the hymn *Lauda Sion* in honor of the Blessed Sacrament; it is recited throughout all of Latin-rite Catholicism on the Feast of Corpus Christi. Thomas invites all the faithful to always deepen their adoration of the Eucharistic Jesus, even though such adoration can never be truly fitting: *quantum potes tantum aude: quia maior omni laude, nec laudare sufficis*. The most beautiful monstrance is still not worthy of the most holy Host. Mary is the living monstrance of Christ, created, sanctified, and glorified by Himself. Yes, without her there

---

19 Bernard of Cluny, *Omni Die Dic Mariae*, "Daily, Daily, Sing to Mary," in the *Birmingham Oratory Hymn Book*, 1854, p. 1202.

would be no Incarnation of Jesus and no real presence in the Blessed Sacrament! Convinced that I can never say enough about the Immaculate, I would dare to apply the words of the *doctor angelicus*, according to Bernard of Cluny, to the Mother of God, to show the impossibility of adequately expressing her greatness. The Latin words of the second stanza of *Lauda Sion* could also be translated into the feminine form: "All thou canst, do thou endeavor: Yet thy praise can equal never such as merits thy great Queen."

The following observations are meant to be "theological lessons" that, in the sense of the above-mentioned theology of St. John, who rested on Jesus's heart, can help us to study Jesus and Mary. They are teachings on the joyful, luminous, sorrowful, and glorious mysteries of the rosary that seek to be a conscious expression of "Marian maximalism," attributing to Jesus's mother always the most outstanding qualities. The quotations of twenty different saints preceding the meditations are, as in a textbook when the author wants to support his opinion with the words of famous writers, references to those who insist upon a joyous and effusive love for Mary. This love is not limited to the minimum as a result of false caution, does not fear misunderstandings and therefore remain silent as a matter of prudence, and does not on account of shallow spirit-mindedness diplomatically deemphasize the greatness that could be expressed about Jesus's mother. Saint Maximilian Kolbe, who sacrificed his life in the concentration camp of Auschwitz to save a man with a wife and children, asks in one of his beautiful Marian prayers to be outdone in his devotion to the Mother of God, so that she is honored and loved even more: "Allow me to give You such glory that no one else has ever given You up to now. Allow others to surpass me in zeal for Your exaltation and me to surpass them, so that by means of such noble rivalry Your glory may increase ever more profoundly, ever more rapidly, ever more intensely as He who has exalted You so indescribably above all other beings Himself desires."

This little "textbook" about the rosary that seeks to be nothing else than a help for the study of the "kneeling theology" is hopefully a contribution to this Maximilian, or let us say "maximalist," competition for the greater glory of Mary.

This may not seem appropriate for the present time, but exactly for this reason it may be a little contribution in this "Marian winter" that dominates in certain places, awakening courage and joy among those who desire to pray the rosary and venerate Jesus's mother. May God grant increasing participation to the "noble competition" of St. Maximilian Kolbe; with him, out of love for Mary, let us outdo each other in honoring her. It is love, as we read from Thomas à Kempis (1380–1471) in *The Imitation of Christ*, that urges never to say enough about Mary, for "love knows no limits, but ardently transcends all bounds. Love feels no burden, takes no account of toil, attempts things beyond its strength; love sees nothing as impossible, for it feels able to achieve all things. . . . Love is watchful, and while resting, never sleeps; weary, it is never exhausted; imprisoned, it is never in bonds; alarmed, it is never afraid." The liturgy of the Church puts in the mouth of Mary the words of the Wisdom of Sirach to make this clear: love of Mary always seeks more and greatness and urges us not to become tired in the competition for her honor and in hoping for the winner's prize. So also say the beautiful words of the Movement of Schönstatt: "*Servus Mariae numquam peribit*—A servant of Mary will never perish"; as she promised her devotees, "I am the mother of fair love. . . . For my spirit is sweeter than honey and my inheritance more delightful than the sweetest honeycomb. . . . Those who eat of me will hunger for more; those who drink of me will thirst for more. Whoever hears me shall not be confounded, and they who operate through me, will not sin. Those who make me known will possess eternal life."[20]

20 Sirach 24:18–31.

PRAYER TO JESUS
FOR AN ALWAYS GREATER LOVE
OF HIS MOTHER MARY

Blessed are You, Jesus, to have Mary!
She, beautiful as the moon and shining like the sun,
is Your mother.
Her eyes are like those of an innocent child,
her lips overflow with words of love,
her bright smile overcomes shadows of fear and sadness.
How often have You said,
"You are so beautiful, there is no stain of sin in you."

Blessed are You, Jesus, to have Mary!
You are the only Son who could have chosen this woman,
who conceived and held Him in her heart,
nourished Him at her breast and caressed Him in her arms.
You left heaven to live in this earthly paradise,
which You had prepared for Yourself.
She is truly Your joy and Your blessing.

Blessed are You, Jesus, to have Mary!
You were able to live for thirty years in the
house of the Virgin
and experience the joy of her closeness.
Although You are the omniscient God, You were pleased
to stay at her side and learn from her.
Yes, as You are the holy God, You took pleasure
in looking at her virtues day after day
and admiring the purity of her life.

She, Your mother, is the only person
who is as perfect and good as You desired.

Blessed are You, Jesus, to have Mary!
When You climbed up to Golgotha's hill,
she was at Your side!
As the first man sought help from the first woman,
You found a new companion as the new Adam
to complete Your work of redemption.
When You looked crying for Your Father
in the darkness of the Cross,
the Mother was there.
When the devil hurt Your heel, she crushed his head,
like a caring woman who crushes with anger a scorpion
that follows her son.

And just in that moment, as they took everything from You,
You gave me Your most precious jewel,
offering me this wonderful woman as mother.
Blessed am I, Jesus, to have Mary!
Through her, O God, You have become my brother.
With her, O Lord, You have redeemed me, a sinner.
She is, O Jesus, our heaven, our blessing, our true joy.
We both, You and I, are truly her children.

I wish I were You, O Jesus.
I am not longing to resurrect the dead,
heal the sick, or walk on stormy waters as You did.
I have no wish to rule over angels and men as You do
and to judge the nations one day.

I do not wish to be praised or glorified,
nor do I wish to be adored and worshipped as God.
No, I just wish to be Jesus
to love our mother as You do.
We both are her children, but only You love her
as she deserves;
You alone give her the proper honor.

I wish I were You, O Jesus,
to love her with the infinite power of a God
who wanted to become dependent on
Mary's love and tenderness.
I wish I were You, O Jesus,
to crown her with all the glories of heaven,
for all that I think and say about her
is always too little compared to
her beauty and greatness.
Yes, I wish so much that I were You, O Jesus,
for I would never again hurt
our mother's heart by my sins.

Jesus,
You preserved Mary from the sins of our first parents
and gave her the richness of Your mercy,
You adorned her soul with all the divine and human virtues
and never let the evil enemy approach her,
even though he tempted You.
You died to lead her, the Immaculate,
into the immortality of heaven.
You raised her up as Queen above angels and men

so that she can reign at Your side forever.
How could I not rejoice over all the great things
You have done for Mary?

Jesus, let me love Your mother and mine as You love her.
Hand me the crown that You want to place on her head.
Say through my mouth all the loving words
You want to tell her.
Use me as Your tool to honor her
in the way that only You can.

Teach me to imitate You perfectly in all that gives her joy.
Lend me Your divine heart so that I can love Mary
and give her mine,
which should belong to her completely as Yours does.
Jesus, grant me the great grace to be truly
a child of Your mother.

Amen

THE JOYFUL MYSTERIES

Jesus Christ, God's only Son, who was conceived by the Holy Spirit and born of the Virgin Mary

Just as Eve, wife of Adam, became by her disobedience the cause of death for herself and the whole human race, so Mary, too, became by her obedience the cause of salvation for herself and the whole human race.

St. Irenaeus of Lyon (130–202)

iat lux—let there be light (Gn 1:3). These are the first words that God says into the nothingness when He begins the work of creation. The Lord says *fiat* ten times, calling into existence space and time, heaven and earth, angels and men, plants and animals. His word creates the visible and invisible reality. He does this out of pure, overflowing love, for no creature can increase His blessedness and greatness but rather each receives, in its own way, part of God's glory.

Fiat—let it be (Lk 1:38). Mary says this word as the angel Gabriel asks for her consent to God's plan in order that the Son of the eternal Father might become the child of a human mother. It is the same great word that formed the entire universe and opened heaven so that the second person of the Most Holy Trinity could descend upon the earth and assume our nature in the Virgin Mary. Mary's word creates the new Adam. Without her there would not be Jesus, who wanted to come to this earth to bring fallen creation back to God. Without her there would not be salvation or redemption. But even if the first Adam had not sinned, there would have appeared a second one to respond as true God and man to the love of the triune God—to respond as only God Himself can. He is the "first-born of the whole creation" (Col 1:15), as for Him all things were created. For the sake of the love that burns in the human soul of Christ, God wanted to call the entire cosmos into existence in order to appear on earth one day. The smallest grain of sand and the brightest seraphim exist for His sake. The *fiat* of the Creator finds its completion in Mary's *fiat*. As the first Eve originates from the first Adam, so the new Adam is formed from the flesh of the new Eve. Jesus and Mary are predestined to be the true crown of creation for eternity, where the light of love shines, not clouded by sins. They are the progenitors of all those who with the strength of grace make their own the great word of Nazareth: *fiat voluntas tua*—let your will be done! (Mt 6:10). He who says this word deeply with an honest heart, as the Lord teaches His disciples to pray, becomes a new creation (cf. 2 Cor 5:17).

Under the Cross Mary became the mother of all those who carry the name of Christ: she does not stop saying the great word of Nazareth whenever we bring her our petitions. She, who is "omnipotent" in her prayers, knows how to stir the heart of God, who grew up so near to her heart when He was a child. She says *fiat*, let it be, and hence it will be. If she prays, heaven obeys her. "For nothing is impossible with God" (Lk 1:37), says the angel. "For nothing is impossible with Mary," we can say with confidence. How can we not affirm this of her, who brought with a single word the Savior into the world?

Jesus, whom you, O Virgin,
took to Elizabeth

This Ark of the Covenant, before which danced David, doesn't it correspond to the Virgin Mary? The Ark of the Covenant kept the stone Tables of the Law. This contained the Law, the second one the Gospel, this the voice of God, the second one the lively word. The Ark of the Covenant shined inside and outside of magnificent gold. Mary shined inside and outside of the light of virginity. The gold of the Ark of the Covenant originated from this world, Mary's one came from Heaven.

St. Maximus of Trier (†349)

ary knows that her relative needs help during the last months preceding the birth of the long-awaited son. She hurries (Lk 1:39), it is said in the Scriptures, through the mountains to assist Elizabeth. Wherever need or danger dominates, wherever pain or difficulties prevail, the Virgin does not hesitate to assist the oppressed. She is the "perpetual help" of all those who need her.

The Mother holds the Son in her womb. As a new Ark of the Covenant, she carries the Lord through the land of the chosen people. Therefore, Mary brings not only help to those in material need but also "Israel's savior," promised by the prophets and awaited also by the last of them, John the Baptist. Full of joy the baby jumped in Elizabeth's womb when encountering the Lord in Mary. As David danced in front of the Ark of the Covenant (2 Sm 6:14–16), the unborn child rejoices in front of the Lord and His mother, who is the true throne of His presence. Where Mary is, there is her child. Who meets her, meets the true God. And all praise she receives as that which came from Elizabeth, who exclaimed in astonishment, "But why am I so favored, that the mother of my Lord should come to me?" (Lk 1:43), for what honors her, honors also the One whom she carries in her womb. She brings to us Christ and all His graces. She is the Mediatrix of the Mediator, whose praises are sung and still have not been silenced today: "My soul magnifies the Lord" (Lk 1:46). Inseparable from this praise to God is that of His mother. Elizabeth intones and Mary confirms it: "From now on all generations will call me blessed" (Lk 1:48), and in a choir of thousands, "Blessed are you among women, and blessed is the child you will bear" (Lk 1:42) is repeated in every Hail Mary over the centuries. Jesus and Mary, the Son of God and His mother, are inseparably united in their mission on earth, in their glory in heaven, in the praise of all those who encounter them with humble faith, as Elizabeth and John did.

He who cannot be contained by heaven rests in Mary's womb. She is the living monstrance, still carrying Christ. He who, as a child, wanted to be brought from her to John, His friend and predecessor, wants to come to me also through her. She is always the path He is on: in this world, in this house, in my soul. Moreover, she is always the way by which I meet Him and the reason my heart begins to leap with joy as David does before the Ark of the Covenant and John in front of Mary. Her image reflects every tabernacle where the Eternal Light burns: here is God.

Jesus, to whom you, O Virgin, gave birth in Bethlehem

Do not be afraid of loving the Blessed Virgin too much. You can never love her enough. And Jesus will be very happy because the Blessed Virgin is His Mother.
St. Therese of the Child Jesus (1873–1897)

inally, the time has come. The long journey is over. Not only that of the young couple of Nazareth, who must go to the town of David because of the Roman census, but also that of Israel, who wandered through the centuries toward the One who was born in a stable. Now that the pagans realize how numerous the Jewish people are, the people of Israel find their true greatness in this most noble child born among them. Finally is born the One who was awaited by Abraham, prefigured by Moses, and announced by the prophets, the One whom every believer hoped to see. The time is fulfilled. The Messiah is here. The eternal enters into history; the Invisible One does not merely enthrone Himself in the Holy of Holies but lies as a little child in the crib, where He is adored not by priests and Levites but by angels and shepherds.

God appears visibly to the people. Since that blessed moment, when He wanted to come to us through Mary, He is here. Shortly before His departure from this world, He made the entire world into "Bethlehem," the "house of bread," which is what the name of the city of David means. He is in innumerable places on this globe, hidden but visible, mysteriously concealed in the form of bread but touchable and literally graspable, silent but also full with words of love that cannot reach the ear but penetrate into the heart. Jesus is here, the true God in the form of an infant, caressed by His mother and recognized by the ones who can see thanks to their belief. Jesus is here, descended as living bread that came down from heaven (Jn 6:15) to keep His promise: "And surely I am with you always, to the very end of the age" (Mt 28:19). Until His return, the Eternal Light will never be extinguished in the "house of bread" and will show the way to Jesus to all those who believe with a simple heart as the shepherds do. "Let's go to Bethlehem" (Lk 2:15), away from the fields of daily work and concerns to the "great joy" (Lk 2:10) that will be given to all the people. He who comes and adores as a poor day laborer the One who, more little and humble than a child in the stable, is truly among us in the small and inconspicuous form of bread, finds this joy. In a manger, where the cattle are fed, lies God's and Mary's Son. He who satisfies the hunger of the angels with His glorious presence wants to give us humans much more—wants to truly be our food. In a crib we find what satisfies our heart.

Mary is the gate through which Jesus wanted to enter our world. Without pain she bore the One who came to take upon Himself all our pains and to break the curse of our first parents (Gn 3:16). The new Eve conceived Jesus with chaste virginity, gave birth without injury or pain, and met Him again in heaven without death. With the birth of the new Adam begins the new creation that arises already gloriously in Mary. She was not overcome with the pains and cries of a pregnant woman (Rv 12:2) in Bethlehem but rather under the Cross—not at the birth of her only child, but at my birth into new life. The arrival of Jesus in this world did not cost her tears, but for my spiritual birth into grace she shed countless ones. The Lord wants me to love her as He loves her because she bore both of us. As a good mother, Mary wants to gather into the "house of bread" the countless souls who so painfully became her children, that they might find their "great joy," Jesus, the King in the crib.

Jesus, whom you, O Virgin,
offered up in the Temple

And just as Adam and Eve sold the world for an apple,
so in a certain sense my Son and I redeemed the world
with one heart.

St. Bridget of Sweden (1303–1373)

he fortieth day after the birth, Mary brings her
Son to the Temple according to the law of
Moses: "born of woman, born under the law"
(Gal 4:4). He who as an infant had rested in the arms of
the Virgin is the One who spoke on Sinai. Now He
comes, as a member of the chosen people, to fulfill completely what had been asked of Israel. The Lord begins His
earthly mission in the sanctuary in Jerusalem "to redeem
those under the law, that we might receive adoption to
sonship" (Gal 4:5). He is not ransomed as firstborn Son—
we are. It is not the sacrifice of animals that makes us
God's children but the devotion of Jesus and Mary, whose
innocence and purity are symbolized by two young
pigeons (Lk 2:24), the gift of the poor (Lv 12:8). Jesus
comes to the Temple carried in the arms of His mother,
not offering any other sacrifice than Himself. He is the
Lamb brought to the altar by His mother. What happens
here in the Temple under the veil of the Mosaic law will
be revealed on the day when this curtain will be torn in
two (Mt 27:51). After that, Jesus will show Himself as the

true Son of Abraham, and in His offering no angel will help His mother to save His life (cf. Gn 22:11–12). Then, the Son will make us sons.

The elderly Simeon recognizes the new that is concealed behind old rituals. His weak eyes see an infant, but his heart recognizes in Him the "salvation" of the world (Lk 2:30). All the sacrifices of the Jewish Temple were only anticipatory images that referred to the One who would come and only had significance and effect in connection with Him, and finally the Lamb that will take away all the sins of the world has appeared (Jn 1:29). Simeon sees, inspired by the Holy Spirit, how this defenseless infant will grow into a man, be nailed to the Cross, and be just as weak and helpless as on this fortieth day after His birth, will then redeem mankind through His death. He will be the bloody sacrifice, whose countless wounds will burn with the same intensity in His mother's soul. It is a sword that will pierce the hearts of Jesus and Mary to make them both, as the two pigeons on the day of the ritual sacrifice, the price of our salvation. Simeon foretells to Mary that the Suffering Servant, promised by the prophets, is her Son, by whose side she will stay when He completes His work on earth. Mary recognizes in this hour that, when the Savior will give His body and life, she should imitate His example with the painful devotion of her soul. She will—what mother would not feel the terrible sword in her heart?—give her consent, like Abraham, to the sacrifice of her Son in fulfillment of God's will. She is bringing Him today to the Temple, and she will accompany Him to Golgotha. For "when Christ came into the world, he said: 'Sacrifice and offering you did not desire, but a body you prepared for me; with burnt offerings and sin offerings you were not pleased.' Then I said, 'Here I am—it is written about me in the scroll—I have come to do your will, my God.'" (Heb 10:5–7).

Jesus has no natural father. His flesh is Mary's flesh. His face bears her features. The One whom she sacrifices in the Temple bears much more resemblance to His mother than every other human child to his. The "sacrifice of the body of Jesus Christ" (Heb 10:10), which saves us, belongs to Mary. She gives Jesus her "flesh and blood" so that I can bear His resemblance and can also be her child. In the faces of Jesus's brothers and sisters, who by the Cross become part of God's family, is reflected also Mary's image, the loving countenance of the Mother.

Jesus, whom you, O Virgin, found in the Temple

I propose myself to keep in me the will to work on turning into Mary, in order to become another Mary, alive and active. I propose myself to be transformed into her and through her to transform my thoughts, my desires, my words, my deeds, my prayers, my sorrows, my entire life and my death.

Charles de Foucauld (1858–1916)

e is not here. Full of sorrows, Mary and Joseph look for their Son whom they cannot find in the group of pilgrims. Not until the third day do they find Him in the Temple. As the Mother embraces the child with joy and does not want to let Him go anymore, there are already signs of the happy hour when the Lord will look for her first after His resurrection, to show her that the One thought to be lost is alive. Then she will remember what He said to her in the Temple: "Didn't you know I had to be in my Father's house?" (Lk 2:49). And she will let Him go again for a while, so that He can return to the One who sent Him.

Mary suffers painfully on account of this separation from her Son and shares, though she is without sin, the fate of those who lose their Lord. In her pure soul Mary tastes the bitterness of being without Jesus and shows the way to those who want to find Him again. Although she is the beloved daughter, who can never be far from God, her Son expects her to hurry, seeking her lost Son, to the house of the Father, to find Him there. Hence, she precedes all those who want to come back home. She, refuge of sinners, becomes guide and leader of all those who are fed in troughs (cf. Lk 15:16), to bring them finally to the One who waits for them with open arms. Mary does not know sin, but she understands the needs of those who have lost Jesus through their sins. She turns to the house of the merciful Father with all those who are repentant. "Son, why have you treated us like this?" (Lk 2:48)— Mary believes in, submits herself to, and grows always deeper in the mysteries of Jesus, who will call Himself "Son of Man" to demonstrate more clearly that she—the Mother—is inseparably connected with His work. The twelve-year-old boy explains God's word to the scribes. He teaches His mother in another way: He expects her to enter always deeper into His mission as Savior through her suffering. She does not need many words, for He revealed Himself to be the true and eternal Word that became flesh in her. He could say to her so much about why He allows this and even worse things to happen to His mother. However, this is not necessary because the obedient woman, who pronounces her *fiat* in the blessed hour of the Incarnation, remains, whatever happens, faithful to her Word. Yes, she remains forever faithful to the eternal Word that is her own. Therefore, Mary is subject to the One who submits Himself to her (Lk 2:51).

She follows Him, led by His hand. They both go out of the Temple down to Nazareth to grow up in the concealment of the little village, waiting for the day when they will return to Jerusalem to fulfill what has been asked of the Messiah.

Mary finds her lost Son. She will also look for me when I follow other paths and eventually find that I am lost; she will take me back to her home. The little Jesus will grow up into a man by Mary's hand. He will also learn from her to increase "in wisdom" (Lk 2:52). He, who could teach the scribes in the Temple, wants to go as man to the school of His mother. He learns from Mary. In Nazareth, Jesus becomes completely Marian. He, the omniscient one, sits at Mary's feet to listen to her—how could I not follow this example? When she speaks to my heart, He will make His voice heard: "Finally you know that you are in your mother's home."

THE LUMINOUS MYSTERIES

Jesus, baptized by John the Baptist

*It can be said that all the saints are the work of the
Blessed Virgin and that a particular devotion to her is
the characteristic they have all in common.*

St. Maximilian Kolbe (1894–1941)

 ultitudes come to the River Jordan to receive
the baptism of forgiveness from John the Baptist. Tax collectors and adulterers, prostitutes
and thieves, violent soldiers and vain merchants gather
around him to finally obtain forgiveness for their sins.
Among these is a completely innocent Man who is not
ashamed of being called "friend of sinners" (Mt 11:19)
and being "numbered with the transgressors" (Mk 15:28).
He who does not need to ask for forgiveness finds Himself
there to receive salvation for them. He does not fear for
His good reputation or His irreproachable behavior. As
He immerses Himself in the waters of the Jordan, He is
lost amidst the crowd of the lost. "God made him who
had no sin to be sin for us" (2 Cor 5:21).

The last prophet of the Old Covenant is the only one
who recognizes among the sinners the Lamb that one day
will lead the righteous ones (cf. Rv 14:13). John sees the
One who unties His sandal straps to enter into the river,
though he should indeed bow and take off his shoes before
the Master, who walks on water (cf. Mt 3:11). The Lord
bows before His servant. Only because Christ receives

this baptism, establishing it in the Church, will it have the power to forgive sins. Only because He goes down will He be able to lead us up. His immersion in the waters of the Jordan is the harbinger of the bloody baptism He will receive on the Cross (Mk 10:38). The Lamb whom the Baptist immerses with trembling hand in the river will be drowned by violence in His own blood. Yet the Lord rises from the floods, and the heavens open. He will resurrect to shake off all the sufferings as He does with the drops of the Jordan's water. "This is my Son, whom I love": this voice from above, which is the answer of the Father to the humility of the Son of Man, will be heard from everyone becoming son of God through baptism—"this is my son, whom I love" (Mt 3:17). How often has Mary also said this word? When she finds out that her child gets baptized with thieves and idle men, she knows that He will soon start what He has come for in this world. She understands that He walked out of the Jordan only to go toward another baptism. She cannot accompany Him yet. But when John will already have been long murdered, she will be at His side. When He dies on the Cross and no voice resounds from heaven, the Mother will know that the word of the centurion is true: "Surely he was the Son of God!" (Mt 27:54). The Father is well pleased with Jesus's readiness to enter into suffering and offer His life. Mary will give her consent to this sacrifice, although it breaks her heart. While Christ bows under the Baptist's hand, she lowers her head and says again, *fiat*.

Jesus and Mary are the only two people who do not need baptism. The Lamb and the Dove have no sin to be purified of, but for this reason they are the ones who must bring salvation to the world and make sinners into saints. Both have been submerged by the roaring floods on Golgotha in order that I might arise and live. Mary took from the hand of her Son the cup that the apostle could not drink (Mk 10:38). She received the baptism from which the disciples fled—under the Cross as blood and water flowed from Jesus's side. All this for me. All this so that she can make me holy.

Jesus, who revealed Himself
at the wedding at Cana

We pray to God for a lot of things and don't receive them. We pray to Mary for a lot and receive it. Why is this so? Not because Mary is more powerful than God, but because this way God wants to honor His Mother.
Alphonsus Maria de Liguori (1696–1787)

 esus performs His first miracle. He transforms water into wine. Three years later His last miracle will occur on earth when He transforms wine into blood. Both times it happens at a wedding. In Cana He is a guest, during the Last Supper He invites others to sit at His table. Now He celebrates the marriage bond of a friend, then He is wed to His Church. He is the Lamb who holds the wedding feast and is united to His bride when she drinks from the cup that the Lord hands her. He is the new and eternal covenant, established in the drinking of His own blood. This is truly the best wine that the Lord saves until the end of His life (cf. Jn 2:10) before He distributes it to His disciples.

Mary is there with Jesus. She expresses her concern for the urgent situation of the bridal couple, who have run out of wine. She does not need to make a request in order to bring help. In this moment the Mother becomes a bride; the woman who bore Jesus becomes His companion. She is the new Eve at the side of the new Adam. Jesus names Mary *woman*. In this way He gives her the old title of the primordial time of creation, with which God foretold the enemy of the serpent (Gn 3:15). Even before Jesus reveals Himself as the Messiah and Lord through the miracle at Cana, He reveals who His mother is. This woman is the new Eve who accompanies the Savior. Jesus knows that the secure and happy life in Nazareth is definitively over when He does what Mary asks Him. He knows that the first sign of the Messiah will lead Him along a way that will end on Golgotha. There He will call Mary again *woman*. He almost wants to delay this moment when He says not to His mother but to the woman, "Woman, why do you involve me?" (Jn 2:4). In this instant Jesus sees the Cross, in front of which He shies away as man, exclaiming, "Mother, why do you involve me with such suffering?" He does not want to go yet: "My hour has not yet come" (Jn 2:4). However, Jesus transforms water into wine for her. He listens to her because He wants to honor His mother in this way. Christ's first miracle saves the wedding feast. His last one will save the souls of those who are invited to the marriage supper of the Lamb (Rv 19:9). Mary's request, which marks the beginning of this so blessed yet so terrible hour, not only resolves the material need of the bridal couple but also heals the spiritual suffering of sinners. The Mother quietly induces the Son to finally show Himself as divine groom. Those lost souls on the street corners will be invited by Him to the wedding feast that has no end. Six great jars of water are transformed by the Lord into delicious wine so that the earthly celebration can last for days, but according to the Jewish custom, it should be seven jars. The last vessel will be His body, from which is poured the true drink of life that is never exhausted and that leads us to a heavenly celebration that never ends.

"Do whatever he tells you" (Jn 2:5). These are the last of Mary's words recorded in the Scriptures. She says this to prepare others for Jesus's first miracle. When His last one occurs, He will use similar words to instruct the apostles to transform again and again wine into His blood: "do this" (Lk 22:19). Mary's mission goes far beyond the wedding at Cana. He, the one who transforms water into wine and bread into His body, can also transform my life and make it similar to His. Help me, "praying omnipotence," that I might do what He says so that this miracle can occur in me.

Jesus, who announced
the kingdom of God

*I know who I have to love after God: it is my Mother, it
is your Mother, it is the Mother of all the people. If you
only knew how lovely and beautiful the Madonna is.
She is the one through whom we have Jesus. She is the
one through whom we receive mercy. What would become
of us poor sinners without this good Mother?*

St. Joseph Benedict Cottolengo (1786–1842)

esus is King. He has come to this world to establish His supremacy. He has founded the Church
in order that His invisible reign of mercy, which
grows in our hearts, can be manifested and extended.
Wherever the Church is that Christ founded on Peter,
there is the divine truth that the Lord entrusted to His
apostles so that they could announce the good news of salvation. Here are all the means that give sanctity and
therefore create and consolidate the kingdom of God in
our souls. Jesus is the new Moses who writes the law of
mercy not on tablets of stone but in hearts of flesh and
blood. He creates a new nation, which He leads through
the desert of this world to the promised land. His disciples should conquer heaven and take possession of the
kingdom that has already begun but that still awaits completion.

Jesus is the Lord. His crown, however, does not shine

with gold and precious stones but rather is made of thorns. He does not wear the purple of the caesars but a mock robe given to Him by pagan soldiers. His throne is the Cross. There He will leave only seven words to His scattered followers before His heart breaks. Before His death on Golgotha He testifies with seven signs that He is the Messiah, whose arrival inaugurates a new kingdom of David. He is God's Son who performs miracles and forgives sins. What He does in a powerful way to the suffering bodies of some ill people He does also as divine doctor for the souls of all those who pray for mercy. Sinners, the possessed, and the sick constitute the court of this King who gives them healing that they might populate His kingdom. The throne speech, that the Cross-nailed Lord on that rock outside the town cannot hold anymore, will be directed from another mountain to His people, the heir of Israel. Surrounded by the disciples, from whom He will choose twelve, Jesus calls blessed the ones who take up their cross and follow Him (Mt 5:1). What His words say will be shown three years later by the traces of blood on His body (cf. Mt 5:3–10):

> Blessed are the poor, says the naked King on the Cross!

> Blessed are those who mourn, says the Lord racked with pain!

> Blessed are the meek, teaches the Omnipotent, who hangs powerless on the Cross.

Blessed are those who hunger and thirst for righteousness, stutters with a burning throat the condemned innocent one.

Blessed are the merciful, professes the one who forgives his executioners, for they do not know what they are doing.

Blessed are the pure in heart, proclaims the Redeemer, from whose side pours blood and water that wash every sin away.

Blessed are the peacemakers, testifies the Savior of the world, whose death has reconciled heaven and earth (Col 1:20).

Blessed are those who are persecuted for their righteousness, teaches the Master to His disciples, who will share in their Lord's fate.

This is the constitution of the kingdom that Christ has established with His Cross. This is the law of the New Covenant.

Mary is the Queen in God's kingdom, not only because she bore Him, the one who "must reign" (1 Cor 15:25), but because she is truly blessed and has fulfilled more than anybody else what the Lord expects from His disciples. She was the only one who did not need to hear her Son's sermon on the mount, but she could not miss the one given on Golgotha. As the King of the thorns defeats the old serpent in the purple of His blood and establishes His supremacy, she stands by Him. In this hour, she becomes the mother of us all. Therefore, she shares in the victory of the King. When we pray to Him "your kingdom come" (Mt 6:10), we want in the same way hers to begin.

Jesus, who was transfigured
on Mount Tabor

He knew his mother in predestination, even before He was born of her, even before as God, He created her, of whom, as man, He was to be created, He knew her as his Mother.

St. Augustine (354–430)

eter, John, and James, the three apostles who on the Mount of Olives will witness Jesus's suffering are now going to see the glory of the Son. The "rock" (Mt 16:18) can see with his own eyes what He professed a few days before through the power of the Spirit: "You are the Messiah, the Son of the living God" (Mt 16:16). And the "sons of thunder" (Mk 3:17), who want to sit on the right and left side of the Master (Mt 20:21), are standing now by His side as He reveals His glory. On Tabor, the beliefs and wishes, hopes and expectations of the disciples are fulfilled in a moment with this vision. They become in the young Church a solid ground for the faith and a thundering testimony for the truth. On this mountain, where it is possible to see the village of Nazareth from a distance, Mary's child reveals Himself as Son of the eternal Father.

Moses and Elijah appear to testify that Jesus is the promised Messiah of whom the Law and the prophets speak. He is the manna in the wilderness, the rock from which water springs, the fire of the bush that does not burn. All that is said in the Mosaic Scriptures speaks of Him and prepares the chosen people for His arrival. Moses, supported by two men, held up his arms in prayer the entire day (Ex 17:8–16) to ensure the victory. Christ will, nailed to the Cross, pray as the High Priest, to triumph over the enemy and, like Elijah, send burning fire from heaven (1 Kgs 17–47), to free the land from all idols. Jesus is the Lord, who has the power to complete what His servants started in the Old Covenant. The disciples of the New Covenant fall at His feet on Tabor, as they will when He shows Himself to His closest followers as the glorious and resurrected King. Peter, without knowing exactly what he should say in this glorious moment, wants to build three tents. He who wants to remain on this mountain will flee from the other one, where indeed the victory must be won. He who exactly six days before rejected the message of Jesus as the Suffering Servant wants now to enjoy forever the glory of God. But this seventh day, when God rested and gave His people refreshment after the effort of the battle, can only start when that Friday is over, when the new Moses wins the bloody battle against the enemies and the true Elijah offers battle to the servants of the demons. Christ will not call the prophets for assistance, as the Pharisees think (Mt 27:47); He Himself accomplishes the work and overcomes the power of evil. It is not possible to stay on Tabor if Golgotha has not yet been climbed. Shelters should not be built until the cornerstone that the builders rejected (Mt 21:42) becomes the foundation stone of God's house.

Probably Mary did not see the bright light on Tabor from the window of her house in Nazareth. She did not have to be there when her Son revealed to the three apostles that He is the Son of God and came into this world to redeem mankind. The Virgin knows the Father of her Son. She knows that the One she carried for nine months is the only-begotten Son of the Omnipotent and rests with Him in eternal love, with no beginning or end. It is her Son of whom the divine voice said, "This is my Son, whom I love" (Mt 17:5). She does not need to hear this word from above, for she feels it incessantly in her heart.

Jesus, who gave us the Eucharist

The venerable Savior sacrificed himself only once on the altar of the cross for the Father, but his holy Mother offered him ten thousand times on the altar of her heart. This heart was like a priest who offering him, offered himself with him. So we can say that this wonderful heart exercised in this sacrifice the function of the priest and, at the same time, was offering and altar. Oh! How much honor we owe this holy priest, how much reverence for this precious offering, how much veneration for this holy altar.

St. Johannes Eudes (1601–1680)

 esus sends the disciples ahead to prepare the Last Supper. In a mysterious way He suggests to them the place to hide Him from Judas, who would betray Him. No one should disturb what will happen there. The hour of the Son of the omnipotent God, which His entire life has led up to, has finally begun. The apostle should seek a man with a jar of water (Lk 22:10) before they follow the One to the banquet, who offers them the drink of life. He attentively chooses a large room furnished with cushions (Lk 22:12). During this evening, when He will not use an earthly cup but a precious chalice of the paschal ritual, the richness that Jesus will dispense does not tolerate modesty or austere frugality or sober affectation. For this last feast, which will endure forever, the Lord spares no expense. The sacrifice of Calvary, which will be celebrated in the glory of heaven, cannot take on the form of a poor meal during this mysterious anticipation on Holy Thursday.

Jesus has been a guest in the houses of sinners many times: they showed Him so much love, hosted Him lavishly, washed His feet, and poured ointment over His head. Now the Lord does not hold a sinners' meal but as a host allows access only to those who wear a festive robe (cf. Mt 22:12). Except for one, they are all pure as they come from a bath of grace. They only need to have their feet washed (Jn 13:9) before approaching the table that through the presence of Jesus becomes an altar. Here the friends of the Galilean are consecrated as priests of the New Covenant. Here the men that followed Him for three years become true apostles, who will be sent to bring Him to the world. From this day on, they will hold His hand whenever they repeat what He teaches them this evening. The true Paschal Lamb, which will be violently slaughtered the next day, offers them mysteriously His body and His blood as food and drink. The vintage, from which tomorrow will be pressed the last drop, sheds already today its blood. The High Priest, who will present in a few hours His disfigured body as an offering, celebrates this preeminent liturgy on the eve of His salvific suffering, empowering His disciples to *do this* until the end of time. Jesus offers Himself to His Father, who looks with pleasure on this new offering that was foretold by the prophets (see Mal 1:11), and at the same time to His friends, who receive Him only with their mouths but also with their hearts. When we draw near to the Eucharist, we are with the apostles in the Cenacle, and we stand with Mary under the Cross and celebrate still today the feast of the angels, who adore the slaughtered Lamb. With the offering of Christ the boundaries of space and time, of heaven and earth disappear, that we all might be united to the body that is offered to us as food. The Holy Mass is Jesus, the child in the Mother's womb, the infant in Bethlehem, the holy priest in the Cenacle, the Redeemer on the Cross, the resurrected conqueror of death, the Lamb who invites us to the wedding.

Mary is not in the Cenacle. She doesn't receive priestly ordination together with the apostles, for on account of her divine motherhood, she can say always what the priest declares only during the most sacred moment of his sacrifice: "this is my body." Jesus is her flesh and blood. She does not stop offering Christ to the world as Mother and Mediatrix, and thus she is always present when the words of the Cenacle make Him truly present. Through her, He comes to our earth; through her, we find the way to Him. The great sacrament of the body and blood of Christ offers us therefore also spiritual closeness to the Mother who is always by her Son.

THE SORROWFUL MYSTERIES

Jesus, who sweat blood for us

You suffered like your Son with the difference that whereas his wounds were distributed over the body, yours were bundled in your heart.

Bernard of Clairvaux (1090–1153)

t all started in a garden: God created man and made him the crown of His creation. Everything went well until he disobeyed the only command God gave him: "You may eat fruit from the trees in the garden, but you must not eat fruit from the tree that is in the middle of the garden or you will die" (Gn 3:3). With this act all of humanity plunges into misfortune: "sin entered the world through one man, and death through sin, and in this way death came to all people, because all sinned" (Rom 5:12).

Again, all starts in a garden: Jesus, the "new Adam," prays in Gethsemane. Fear of the forthcoming suffering—He knows perfectly the agonies that await Him—forces sweat and blood from His pores. The serpent is there, showing the sweet fruit of freedom and hissing that this death will be so useless for so many people who will reject His love. Jesus wants to atone for what Adam and his children have done in disobeying God to "become like God" (Gn 3:5). He who is God wanted to be man to fulfill the Father's will. Instead of picking the delicious fruit, He wants to drink the bitter chalice. Yet it is so hard. Like any other man, Christ fears suffering and death, and as God's Son He recognizes with complete clarity what lies ahead for Him in the coming hours. He also knows with that mysterious foreknowledge that belongs only to God that for some people His blood will be shed in vain. It is not only the fear of pain and suffering that tortures Him but also the temptation to despair. The almighty God, who created everything, trembles as a weak human before the work of salvation, whose significance will depend upon a *yes* from each soul. In this hour in Gethsemane He sees and knows the decision of every single person. With divine foresight, He sees me too. And as He looks at me lovingly, He willingly embraces the Cross. He is ready to die, not for all people as an anonymous mass of unknown creatures, but for every single person as a beloved child whom He has known from eternity.

Mary, who could comfort Jesus as no other, is not in the garden. However, the Lord thinks in this moment of decision also about her. She is the new Eve by His side, who, as the angel came to her, pronounced her *fiat*— "May your word to me be fulfilled" (Lk 1:38). She will not take back these words even during the terrible hours that are approaching. How she wished she could relieve His suffering! All that His body and soul endure—fear, pain, death—she bears in her heart. As an angel appears from heaven to give Him new strength (Lk 22:43)—was it perhaps the heavenly messenger from Nazareth?—the Lord repeats the word of His mother: *fiat!*

Jesus, who was scourged for us

*Through the blood, that comes from Mary, the world
has been redeemed. Without Mary there would not exist
a Paradise. Without Mary there would not be God for
me. Without Mary there would not exist the magnificent
Heaven, as so many places would have remained empty.*[1]

St. Mary Magdalene of Pazzi (1566–1607)

Pilate knows that Jesus is innocent, but he does
not dare to set Him free. As he orders Jesus to
be scourged, he hopes to quench in this way the
people's thirst for blood, for they have requested a sentence of death. The cowardice of the governor, who seeks
a solution through false compromise, not only brings the
Lord to the Cross but also causes Him to suffer inexpressible pain before His actual execution. Jesus had just said to
Pilate that He "was born and came into the world to testify
to the truth" (Jn 18:37). The Roman official stands against
this truth, and with him all the people who believe that a
"lesser evil" can prevent a greater one or a "little injustice"
a worse one. How often has the fear of public opinion
since the time of Pilate been disguised as diplomacy and
readiness to compromise?

---

1 If the Son of God had not become incarnate thanks to Mary's
fiat, we would not know Jesus, and nothing about the Trinity.

The pagan executioners use their whips to make their prisoner feel that He is not a king and certainly not a God, but only a miserable man. Soon the strokes of the soldiers mercilessly tear at Jesus's body. Again and again they lash His back and His legs. He stands at the column of flagellation as a lamb that is not spared by the slaughterer (cf. Rv 5:6). Why must He endure this torture? Why all this terrible pain? Is His death—the agonizing death of the Cross—not horrible enough? The paved floor surrounding the infamous column turns red with blood. A single drop would have been enough to redeem the world, but Jesus wants to offer Himself completely. In the terror of the flagellation is manifested the mystery of divine love, which always gives more than the creature deserves. Bound to a column, He wants to bind us to Him with "ties of love" (Hos 11:4). Each of the innumerable wounds of the scourged one is a resounding declaration of this love, which endures all this in the hope of finally being loved in return: "Look, God loves you so much!"

The Virgin Mary, who waits with all the people for the pronouncement of the verdict, hears from afar the cries of her Son, who is all but utterly broken by this brutality. She knows what they are doing to Him. She cannot free Him from the hand of His torturers. Each stroke that falls upon Jesus lacerates His heart. And yet she knows the greater mystery hidden in all this suffering, to which she agrees for the sake of our salvation. She knows, perhaps as no one else can during this dark hour, that the cries of pain from her child are the loving summons of a God who truly does everything to draw His creatures to Himself.

Jesus, who was crowned
with thorns for us

God gives to those whom he wishes to save the mercy of a particular devotion to Mary.

　　　　　　　　　　St. John of Damascus (676–749)

aughing and jeering, the Roman soldiers push a crown of thorns onto Jesus's head. Blood flows immediately over the numerous wounds of His head, disfiguring His face, upon which they cast mockery and spittle. "Hail, king of the Jews!" (Jn 19:3) they call out to Him, bowing down before Him. Scribes and Pharisees accuse Jesus, telling Pilate that He has made Himself a king (Jn 19:12). Now the soldiers use this accusation to mock and humiliate the miserable figure before them. Neither the Jews nor the Romans believe that this man from Nazareth is really a king, or even more, the Lord of lords. He who is crowned with thorns, in front of whom the tormentors make mock reverence, is the One before whom Moses prostrated himself as the burning bush spoke to him. He is "before Abraham was born" (Jn 8:58). He is the Son of God. He is the King.

Jesus allows this to happen—allows them to strike Him and spit upon Him, to insult Him and mock Him. The hour has not yet come when He will "sit on the throne of his glory" (Mt 25:31) and pronounce His judgment as

King, calling His followers back: "Come, you who are blessed by my Father; take your inheritance, the kingdom prepared for you since the creation of the world" (Mt 25:34). Then He will pronounce His judgment about what they did for the least of His brothers (Mt 25:40). In this world the weak are abused, the helpless pushed away, the innocent derided. Jesus's kingdom is not of this world, otherwise He would not endure all this suffering and bitter malice, but rather would order His people to free Him by force from Pilate's imprisonment (Jn 18:19). He who in the courtyard of the praetorium recognizes the Omnipotent in the bloody figure of the Nazarene, the One who wanted to make Himself one of the least, he belongs to Him. He who looking at the One crowned with thorns begins to suspect that this King will not establish his kingdom with violence but with the power of love, will hear His call and understand: "Whoever wants to be my disciple must deny themselves and take up their cross and follow me" (Mt 16:24). Under the eyes of Pilate the mocked King begins to recruit His army.

His mother does not see what the soldiers do to Jesus in the courtyard. Only when the Roman governor shows to the people the One who has been condemned to death—*ecce homo!*, behold the man—does she see Him. Her suffocated cry—"look at my child"—gets lost in the commotion. Like no one else she suffers at the sight of her scourged Son, and the Mother is now also His consort. She accompanies the King, crowned with thorns, and is there with everyone who follows Him on the way to the Cross. He who follows her along this path of suffering finds salvation and redemption.

Jesus, who carried the
heavy Cross for us

*For both of you lies an entire army of suffering ahead,
the entire world will conspire against you. God intended
it for good for you to drink from the chalice, and the
Mother should feel the pain she escaped during the birth
of her Son. It is as if she should die with her Son.*

Peter Canisius (1521–1597)

he soldiers placed a cross on Jesus's shoulders.
He goes staggering toward His death. His burden is extremely heavy. He carries not only the
rough wood of the Cross but all of humanity, each person—He carries me. The crowds of onlookers see a criminal who gropes His way to execution. And yet, He is the
Redeemer, as the prophets foretold: "I will place on his
shoulder [the cross as] the key to the house of David" (Is
22:22). With this key, with the Cross, He will open the
gates of heaven. Jesus goes not toward the tragic end of a
condemned man but to a sacrificial death by which He
will redeem the world. He goes up to Golgotha, entering
as High Priest: "he did not enter by means of the blood of
goats and calves; but he entered the Most Holy Place once
for all by his own blood, thus obtaining eternal redemption" (Heb 9:12).

Jesus falls several times on His way to Calvary. The liturgy that He will celebrate as High Priest until the veil in the Temple of the Old Covenant is torn is hidden under sweat, blood, and tears. Who could really understand what Jesus does on the way to the Cross? The Lord Himself, although He wants to fulfill His Father's will, relies on the help of a stranger, who carries the Cross with Him. Without him, without me, to carry with Him this burden, He cannot reach His goal. On this steep way to Calvary, the suffering—especially these bitter agonies that cannot be endured with the serenity of a shining hero or the stoic tranquility of an ascetic—becomes the key to heaven. Since Jesus has taken the Cross on His shoulders, no pain is senseless if it is shared with Him. The women of Jerusalem stand by the wayside and weep at the sight of the condemned man. Perhaps they think about their own children, whom they wish to save from such a terrible fate. They remain spectators. Their tears cannot comfort Jesus because they do not go with Him. They do not carry His Cross. They are dry wood through which does not pass the sap of passionate love and active mercy. "Weep for yourselves and for your children" (Lk 23:28), so that your hearts open and become truly compassionate, "for I desire steadfast love" (Hos 6:6), not useless complaints and agitated crying that become silent as soon as the horrible spectacle of the execution is over.

Mary meets Jesus on the way to the Cross. Silently she repeats the words she said once, when she found Him in the Temple after three days of sorrow: "Son, why have you treated us like this?" (Lk 2:48). She is a woman who suffers because she sees her only Son going to the place of execution. She knows that He will live only a few more hours, and these will be filled with incredible suffering. She goes with Him, for He needs her—not only as a mother who always knows how to comfort, but as companion to the Redeemer who will stand at His side in that hour which was foretold at Cana (Jn 2:4). When the High Priest upon the Cross will pour forth the wine of the New Covenant, she will be with Him to offer it to those who accompanied Him on the arduous ascent to Golgotha.

Jesus, who was crucified for us

O Mary, bearer of fire, Mary, fruitful land, Mary, restorer of human generation, because the world was repurchased by means of the sustenance that your flesh found in the Word. Christ repurchased the world with His Passion, and you with your suffering of mind and body.

St. Catherine of Siena (1347–1380)

 he soldiers tear Jesus's clothes off His body, pull Him over to the rough Cross and pound merciless nails into His hands and feet. Then they straighten up the post on which the Lord will die. "Who is hung on a pole is under God's curse" (Dt 21:23), says the law of Moses. The scribes spit scornfully in front the supposed Messiah, who takes His last breaths on the Cross before their eyes. From their point of view He is a failed fraud, whose end reveals who He really was: one cursed by God. It is the serpent named in the first book of the Bible that snaps at Jesus and bites inexorably. But it strikes only His heel (Gn 3:15). Exactly in this moment, when everything seems lost and darkness literally covers the earth (Mt 27:45), the Lord fulfills His mission on earth: the redemption of the world.

Everything is dark—so dark that Jesus cannot even see His Father: "My God, my God, why have you forsaken me?" (Mt 27:46). Worse than the wounds of His mistreated body is the pain of His human soul, which must endure what it is to be far from God. On the other hand, just in this night of God's apparent absence, "the rising sun will come to us from heaven to shine on those living in darkness and in the shadow of death" (Lk 1:79). Jesus's love goes so far that He takes on Himself the estrangement of sinners to bring them again to the closeness of the Father. His yearning for God is theirs and does not remain unheard by Him. The bystanders don't understand what Jesus says in Hebrew, the language of the Temple: "Eli, Eli, lema sabachtani!" (Mt 27:46); they think He implores the help of Elijah. It is instead the first verse of Psalm 22, which describes the suffering of the Messiah. "Dogs surround me, a pack of villains encircles me; they pierce my hands and my feet" (Ps 22:16). In this moment occurs that which was foretold by David: "They divide my clothes among them and cast lots for my garments" (Ps 22:19). The Lord did not appear as a poor itinerant preacher on Golgotha but rather was dressed as a king, a high priest, whose precious robe was without seam. Perhaps Jesus prays silently Psalm 22 as the evening prayer of the only true Levite. The last words of the Lord before death—"it is finished" (Jn 19:30)—recall the end of this prayer: "he has done it!" (Ps 22:32). The work of our redemption is consummated.

The Mother of Sorrows stands by Jesus under the Cross. Psalm 22 speaks also about her: "From birth I was cast on you; from my mother's womb you have been my

God" (Ps 22:10). If the Lord had these words in mind while He was dying, He may have looked upon Mary at this moment. She who was closest to Him on earth and held Him so often in her arms is offered now as mother to John, and also to me. He gives His mother as the last gift of His earthly life, so that I might always be safe in her embrace. This is His testament, His sacred bequest. She wishes to be the mother of everyone, as she is of her only Son.

THE GLORIOUS MYSTERIES

Jesus, who rose from the dead

The Good Lord could have created a more beautiful world than this one, but he could not have created a more perfect creature than Mary.

St. John Vianney, Curé of Ars (1786–1859)

n the seventh day [God] rested from all His work" (Gn 2:2), but finally the Lord has awoken. Even before the morning star appears, all trace of death has left Him. On this first day of the week truly begins the new creation in which death is forever conquered (see Is 25:8). The longest Sabbath in history is over. Jesus, who shed blood on the Cross for the remission of sins and descended into the land of the dead to proclaim the good news of the coming liberation (1 Pt 4:6), has completed His work: "it is finished!" (Jn 19:30).

And yet exactly on this first day the new work begins. In a garden the first man was created. In a garden the new Adam rises from the dead. Mary Magdalene sees Jesus and thinks it is the gardener (Jn 20:15). She is not wrong. The resurrected one begins to create a new paradise. It will not be of this world, as was the first one, but the plants He wants to set out in His heavenly garden are grown here on earth. He is the divine gardener who sows the seeds, waters them, and takes care of them, that they might mature and find a place in His kingdom. There the seed becomes a tree that never withers and always bears abundant fruit (Rv 22:2). The good gardener knows that dry or stony soil weakens the seeds and that weeds are growing wildly, threatening to suffocate the little plants (cf. Mk 4:1–9). The grain of wheat that had to die[2] blew up the rock tomb. The little kernel that was cruelly threshed by the soldiers, ground by the hard wood of the Cross, and then buried in a dark tomb grew vigorously out into the brightness of a new day. The hard stone, where death reigned, was broken into a thousand pieces and became fertile soil teeming with life. The Lord distributes this rich earth so that His fields and vineyards will flourish. What the divine gardener sows into this soil will not wither in the heat of the day or suffocate under a tangle of ivy, the poisonous plant of the cemetery. The new creation has begun and, since that Sunday morning, has continued to grow toward eternal life. A new garden will appear, even more beautiful than the original one that we lost. The resurrected one is the firstborn of this "new earth" (Rv 21:1). In this paradise "there will be no more death or mourning or crying or pain, for the old order of things has passed away" (Rv 21:4).

The most beautiful flower in this new garden is Mary. She is the "perfect world," as perfect as God wanted; she is

---

2 Very truly I tell you, unless a kernel of wheat falls to the ground and dies, it remains only a single seed. But if it dies, it produces many seeds (Jn 12:24).

His paradise, which is "full of mercy." From the moment of her conception, the divine gardener has cared for her as for no other. No weeds, worms, or insects have ever blighted this beautiful rose. The redemption that Christ has obtained for men through His death and resurrection was not for her release from the guilt of sin, but for her preservation and sanctification. Mary and Jesus are the last flowers of the earthly paradise that remained with us from the lost kingdom of innocence. Mary and Jesus are the first and most beautiful flowers of the new garden of God, in which, by His grace, we too will grow and flourish.

Jesus, who ascended into heaven

All the gifts, all the mercies, all the heavenly effects come from Christ, the head, and reach the body of the Church through Mary as through the neck. Mary the virginal Mother, is the closest one to the head. Her task is to unite the body with the head. A member, who wants to experience the life-giving influence of the head, but refuses to get it through the neck, would completely dry out and die.

St. Robert Bellarmine (1542–1621)

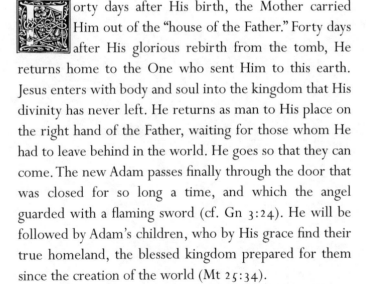orty days after His birth, the Mother carried Him out of the "house of the Father." Forty days after His glorious rebirth from the tomb, He returns home to the One who sent Him to this earth. Jesus enters with body and soul into the kingdom that His divinity has never left. He returns as man to His place on the right hand of the Father, waiting for those whom He had to leave behind in the world. He goes so that they can come. The new Adam passes finally through the door that was closed for so long a time, and which the angel guarded with a flaming sword (cf. Gn 3:24). He will be followed by Adam's children, who by His grace find their true homeland, the blessed kingdom prepared for them since the creation of the world (Mt 25:34).

Jesus says farewell to His followers. Mary and the apostles are with Him when He begins to ascend to His

Father's house. With His last words, He sends them into the world so that what He has done might reach every man: "you will be my witnesses . . . to the ends of the earth" (Acts 1:8). The task Jesus bestows upon His disciples, especially in the moment of His return to the Father, is a true one-way mission. He wants His disciples to be witnesses—the Greek word of the Scriptures means "martyrs," for they will preach the gospel to all creatures not only with their example and words but also with their blood. With the water of baptism and the blood of the Eucharist grows the Church, which the faithful throughout the centuries continue to water with their tears and nourish with their blood. The sacrifice of the Redeemer persists in the members of His mystical body, who continue His work on earth and fill up what is lacking in the sufferings of Christ (Col 1:24). Jesus therefore entrusts His Church to the men of Galilee, who look with astonishment up to the sky (Acts 1:11). If they always keep their gaze toward heaven, they will not forget or neglect their mission. For this reason, Mary remains with them on earth, though she would like to stay forever with her Son. But the young Church needs her. Through her the apostles will understand what they must do. She bore the head of the Church; she is the first of His disciples who walked all the way with Him; she redeemed the world with Him and supported with bitter pains His mystical body at the foot of the Cross. Now she must hold the infant in her arms as "Mother of the Church" and nourish it with the sweet milk of Christ's teaching, until it can stand on its own feet. She is the life-giving connection between it and the members of His body. Jesus goes to the Father, but the Mother stays, in order to be there when the young Church takes its first steps.

But our citizenship is in heaven" (Phil 3:20). Jesus had to leave this earthly reality to lead us into the celestial one. He does not want to establish a paradise on earth but rather holds open the door that He first passed through. Beyond that gate, He prepared a place for me. In the "house of the Father" there is a room (Jn 14:2) that waits for me. There I will be truly at home. In this valley of tears it is Mary who will lead me there. Where her Son Jesus is, may I also live forever as her child.

Jesus, who sent the Holy Spirit

God, the Holy Spirit, who does not produce any divine person, became fruitful through Mary whom he espoused. It was with her, in her and of her that he produced his masterpiece, the God-made-man, and that he produces every day until the end of the world the members of the body of this adorable Head. For this reason the more he finds Mary his dear and inseparable spouse in a soul, the more powerful and effective he becomes in producing Jesus Christ in that soul and that soul in Jesus Christ.

 St. Louis-Marie Grignion de Montfort (1673–1716)

od's spirit visited the prophet Elijah with a gentle blowing of the wind (1 Kgs 19:12). But now that the New Covenant has begun and the Church must show itself to the world as the beautiful bride of the Lamb, the Spirit comes with a mighty wind and tongues of fire. The doors that the apostles closed for fear of the Jews are burst open so that the young Church can step out into the world. The Holy Ghost vivifies the hidden seed and immediately brings forth an abundant harvest: "that day there were added about three thousand souls" (Acts 2:41).

In the solitude of Nazareth the Holy Ghost formed in Mary's womb the God-Man, and on the night before His suffering the Spirit made present among the apostles the true body of the Lord. Now He comes again to make Christ present not in the Eucharist but in His mystical body. It is His mission in the world to create the body of the Lord. The divine Spirit that Jesus breathed forth from the Cross is on the day of Pentecost the great wind that transforms frightened men into a militant Church that fearlessly steps out into the world. He is fire falling from heaven that enkindles under the heart of the Virgin the "light of the world" and fills in the Cenacle the precious chalice with blood radiating the fire of love—blood that Christ would shed the next day unto the last drop. He now inflames the hearts of the disciples so that they glow in the darkness. The Lord once prohibited them from commanding fire to fall from heaven (Lk 9:54), but now they themselves will become flaming torches setting the earth alight (cf. Lk 12:49). He who dwelled in Mary's womb and is inconspicuously present in the form of bread establishes on the day of Pentecost this glorious kingdom. His mystical body appears visible in the world and grows through the testimony and the miraculous signs of His members. Today the Lamb is the roaring lion in the thunder of the Holy Spirit, and He has come to conquer the whole world. Today His bride is a queen, and thus will she remain, throughout all the persecutions and sufferings, until the day she will call the last of her children together in the Spirit: "Come!" (Rv 22:17).

The bystanders thought the exulting disciples had drunk too much wine. The Lord has poured out His spirit. The "mother of fair love" (Sir 24:18), who is filled with the Holy Spirit, becomes the overflowing jar of the divine breath. Through her, Christ stepped into the world; through her, the Holy Ghost flows over everyone who prays with Mary for His glorious return. Mary is the chalice from which we partake of the abundance of divine grace. She is the vessel overflowing with God's love (cf. Rom 5:5). The bride of the Spirit lets us taste the sweetness of this new wine. "They that drink me shall yet be thirsty" (Sir 24:21). He who takes only a sip can nonetheless imagine the greatness that God has prepared for those who love Him (1 Cor 2:9).

Jesus, by whom you were assumed,
O Virgin, into heaven

I strongly wish to die in order to live with Mary. Recite
a Hail Mary for me. Obtain for me the grace to die now
in this pulpit. I want to go see Mary.
                    St. Leonard of Port Maurice (1676–1751)

ary did not die. She who from the first moment
of her existence was free from sin did not see in
the last moment of her earthly life its bitter
fruit—death (Rom 6:23). Her return home occurred as
God wanted it to be for Adam and Eve, who instead
brought death into the world. The new Adam died on the
Cross so that the original plan of the Creator would be
fulfilled for the new Eve, who was preserved from the
baleful effects of the primordial sin. At least one human
being lived on this earth without sin and departed from it
without death. At least once there was a love so strong
and pure that it not only raised a soul to God but also tore
with ecstatic force the body from the narrowness of this
world. At least once the serpent could not bite the heel—
for even Christ allowed Himself be thus afflicted for the
sake of our salvation. Mary's perfection of unity of body
and soul is the complete victory over an old enemy under
whose power death remains (see Heb 2:14).

Mary endured death. On Golgotha she experienced

fear and pain that could not have been worse if she had been nailed to the wood of the Cross instead of her Son. Mary went through hell. God dies before her eyes, and only darkness remains where the demonic mockery and laughing of the executioners echoes. But nevertheless she never stopped believing and loving. For three hours Christ hung on the Cross. The Son freed Mary's martyred soul from the burning nails only on the third day. As no one else she deserved to ascend with Jesus to heaven and to be finally forever with Him. But again, her hour on earth lasts longer than the time of the Lord, and it seems as if she is still held painfully and cannot go; but now no bitter suffering reaches the Mother's heart, for she knows that her Son lives. No sorrow afflicts her soul, for the presence of her Son comforts her. He is there, in the body of the young Church, on the altar of the apostles, in the heart of the Mother. What tortures Mary is the pain of the longing for heaven and the weight of the chains that bind her to this world. Love tortures the daughter who is longing for the house of the Father, the bride who longs to embrace her beloved, the Mother who misses her child and dreams about His radiant smile. Amidst this both painful and sweet love, which only becomes stronger until the blessed day of her deathless return home, the Lord leaves His mother behind on earth. Thus He gave the Church a heart that will always beat stronger and more passionately in order to bring His blood, His divine mercy, to all the members of His mystical body. This immaculate heart has never stopped beating. Never has it been broken. The divine fisherman caught her heart with His fishing rod and began to draw it always nearer to Him. The power of this love eventually reached to such a degree that Christ pulled Mary out of the floods of this world and brought her to the sweet refuge of dry land. He did not bring death but true love; not the downfall but the ascent; not the end but the beginning. In an ecstasy of intense longing Mary has entered into love with body and soul.

Where the Mother is, love reigns. Where Mary is, there is heaven. To follow her means to reach that blessed place where she awaits us and prepares a place for us. There she wants to show us Jesus, the fruit of her body. The Immaculate did not need to fear the last hour of her life; rather, she was longing for it. We ask her again and again to step into our life at its two most important moments: now and the hour of our death. May I be ever calling upon the mercy of the Lord, so that I will not fear the step to the other side, where all is transformed into glory.

Jesus, who crowned you,
O Virgin, in heaven

I wish I could love her as much as she deserves. But remember that all the saints and angels together cannot love and praise the Mother of God according to her worth.

St. Pio of Pietrelcina (1887–1968)

he One who covers Himself with light as with a garment (Ps 104:2) has clothed His mother with the sun (Rv 12:1). Mary stands, shining brightly, on the right hand of the Son (Ps 45:10): the Queen at the side of the King, the Mediatrix by the Mediator, the Lady by the Lord, our Salvatrix by the Savior of the human race. What Christ possesses by virtue of His divine nature He gives to Mary, to the extent that a creature can receive it. He places upon her head a ring of stars to make her the crown of all creation. The human Mother of God, in whom He wished to remain hidden for nine months, shines in the brightness of His glory, in which she is now immersed forever. She is the immaculate mirror in which the Trinity sees a reflection of Itself. She is the joy of the divine Persons who thanks to Their beatitude do not need any creatures. She is the Princess of love, the chosen one of God.

Mary is as Queen the "the great sign" (Rv 12:1) of the

coming victory. She walks upon the moon, the star of the night, with her feet, glowing in the darkness for the pilgrim instead of the moon. She is the Church in a state of perfection and triumphant celebration. Wherever her light breaks through the blanket of clouds, the people of God, though they are still fighting, rejoice—for they know that the Virgin's foot has crushed the dragon. Amidst this fight to the death, his murderous tail cannot strike those who flee under the mantle of the warrior Queen. The humble Virgin of Nazareth has become the noble Lady of heaven and earth who leads her troops to victory. She does not merely recline on her throne among the seraphim but descends to the desert in order to intervene as the mother of all nations. She is the strong woman who cuts off the head of the enemy, and like Judith, embarrasses the helpless men. She is the powerful fighter whose weapons are grace and mercy. It is she who allows the Church to stride triumphantly, with head held high, through the enemy forces. The Queen of Heaven wants to extend her rule to earth. Through her, with her, and in her, the kingdom of Christ spreads in this world, to come to perfection when the Mother of the Lamb holds her child over the throne, when she will bring Him all those who followed Him in the pains of this life. Mary's children will populate heaven and live among the angels, who acknowledge one of Adam's daughters as their Lady. The fallen spirits, who in their pride cannot accept that a human being is daughter, mother, and bride of their God and reigns as true Queen over them, testify to Mary's power by their incessant growling in the darkness.

Mary is my mother; may she show us that she is the Queen! It is impossible for angels and men to ever adequately praise a creature who is so intimately immersed in the adorable Trinity. Our praise for this sublime woman is always too little. Only He, who crowned Mary with such love, is able to honor the one who is the crown of all creation.

Prayer of Consecration
to the Blessed Virgin Mary

No one goes to the Father but by the Son;
no one goes to Christ but by you, O Mary.[1]
No one is heard when you do not intercede for him,
and no one receives mercy and salvation
unless through you.[2]
As the eternal Word wanted to be completely yours
and to come into this world through you,
so I also want to belong entirely to you,
and find through you, Gate of Heaven, eternal life.[3]

Therefore I choose you, O Mary, as my
mother and Queen.
I surrender myself to you as your eternal
possession and property.

1 Pope Leo XIII, *Octobri Mense*: "Thus as no man goeth to the Father but by the Son, so no man goeth to Christ but by His Mother."

2 Pope Leo XIII, *Augustissimae Virginis Mariae*: "For so great is her dignity, so great her favor before God, that whosoever in his need will not have recourse to her is trying to fly without wings."

3 St. Louis-Marie Grignion de Montfort, *True Devotion to the Blessed Virgin Mary*: "It was through the Blessed Virgin Mary that Jesus came into the world, and it is also through her that he must reign in the world."

Let my name
be deeply inscribed in your immaculate heart,
which has never stopped beating
with love for God and for us men.[4]

I consecrate and give to you
my body and my soul with my internal
and external possessions,
with all that I am and have.
Yes, even the value of all my good actions,
past, present, and future, belong only to you.
Totus tuus!—I am completely yours, O Mary!

Accept me, even though I am a poor sinner,
as your child,
as your servant,
as your possession
that you desire to protect and save.

Without any exception you have the right
to dispose of me and everything that belongs to me
according to your will.

4 Bl. John Henry Newman: "Who can conceive that that virginal frame, which never sinned, was to undergo the death of a sinner? Why should she share the curse of Adam, who had no share in his fall?" See also St. Bonaventura, *Sent.* III, d. 3, p 1, a. 1, q. 2: "If the Blessed Virgin was free from the Original sin, then she couldn't be subjected to death."

Let me be an instrument in your immaculate hands
that you use as you want,
for God's greater glory and for the salvation of souls.
Wherever you are loved and adored,
Christ's glory increases and His Church blossoms.[5]

O Mary,
show in my weakness your power,
which you have received from God
as refuge of sinners and Mediatrix of all graces.[6]
Show yourself as Mother and Salvatrix,
and extend through me the kingdom of your Son—
may He reign as Lord and King.

Amen

5 St. Louis-Marie Grignion de Montfort, *The Secret of Mary*: "We must place ourselves as an instrument in Mary's hands, for her to act in us and do with us and for us whatever she pleases for the greater glory of her Son and through the Son, for the glory of the Father."

6 Pope Leo XIII, *Jucunda Semper*: "The deepest reason why we look for the protection of Mary through the prayers, is most certainly her office as mediator of divine grace. She always administers this office by God as she possesses thanks to her dignity and her merit his greatest pleasure and is surpasses with regard to power all the saints in heaven." The recourse we have to Mary in prayer follows upon the office she continuously fills by the side of the throne of God as Mediatrix of Divine grace; being by worthiness and by merit most acceptable to Him, and, therefore, surpassing in power all the angels and saints in Heaven.

By the same author

Totus Tuus, Maria: Personal Consecration to Our Lady Following the Spiritual Teaching of St. Louis-Marie Grignion de Montfort

Pope St. John Paul II chose Totus Tuus as his apostolic motto. A Latin phrase meaning "totally yours," it expressed his personal consecration to Mary, based on the spiritual teaching of St. Louis-Marie Grignion de Montfort and the Mariology of his writings. The saintly pontiff defined it as an expression of piety but also of devotion, deeply rooted in the mystery of the Blessed Trinity. Saint Louis-Marie Grignion de Montfort showed that there is a sure way that leads to Jesus Christ; this way is Mary. In *Totus Tuus, Maria*, commissioned by the Institutum Marianum of Regensburg and first published in German in 2002, Msgr. Florian Kolfhaus recovers the intention of St. Louis-Marie Grignion de Montfort and presents it in a way appropriate for the readers of our day. This text invites the reader to follow this path to sanctity. It cannot be simply read; rather, one must pray with it and meditate upon it, so that it can lead, step by step, to the consecration to Mary. Whoever offers himself up to Mary through this consecration to her seeks shelter under the protective mantle of the Virgin, as Jesus Christ Himself did, and tries to model his life according to her example of charity and love for God. Is there something more perfect that we can do in our earthly life and for our eternal salvation? The reader will find himself in the company of those whom the book presents in nine short biographies: saints, like Pope St. John Paul II, who have found the fullness of life in Jesus Christ through consecration to Mary.

Via Dolorosa: Meditations on the Via Crucis

Jesus suffers because He wants to teach us to love. He calls us to embrace the Cross, because He seeks our friendship. Praying the way of the Cross is not merely an expression of piety that brings tears to the eyes of a pious soul, contemplating—from a safe distance—the suffering of Jesus and one's neighbor. No, it is an invitation to follow the same path. The goal is to let Jesus speak to me personally, then to walk the *via dolorosa* of my own life. With Him, this sorrowful way transforms into the *via amorosa*, a loving path, at the end of which I can discern that no suffering is meaningless if it is accepted with even one spark of love. Life is not about living "by the skin of one's teeth" but rather "finding salvation."

Made in the USA
San Bernardino, CA
21 November 2018